DOT-TO-DOT

FAMOUS PLACES

PULL-OUT PERFORATED PAGES

TEST YOUR BRAIN AND DE-STRESS WITH PUZZLE SOLVING AND COLORING

PaRragon

Bath • New York • Cologne • Melbourne • Delhi
Hong Kong • Shenzhen • Singapore

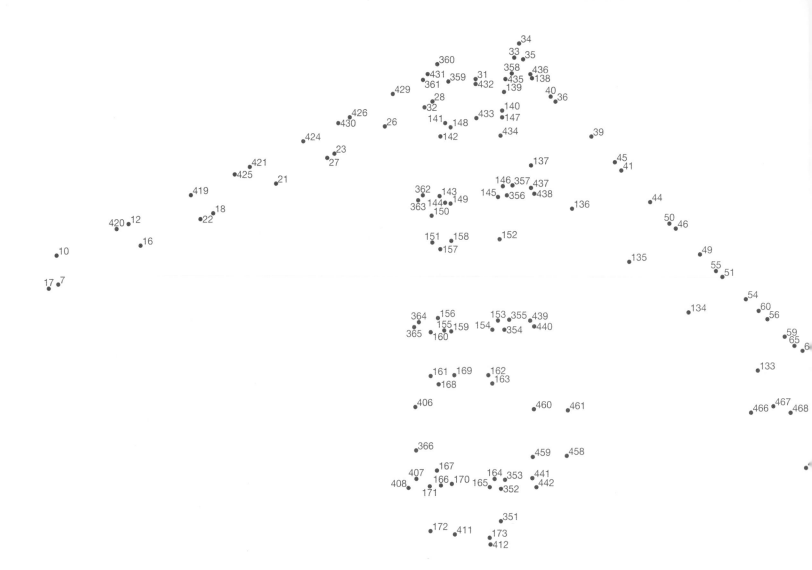

This edition published by Parragon Books Ltd in 2017

Parragon Inc.
440 Park Avenue South, 13th Floor
New York, NY 10016
www.parragon.com

Copyright © Parragon Books Ltd 2017

Puzzles created by Any Puzzle Media Ltd

ISBN 978-1-4748-5866-3

Printed in China

HOW TO USE THIS BOOK

If you love an engrossing puzzle and revel in the distinctive landmarks of the world, here is the perfect challenge. As you move from page to page, you can outline Gaudi's emblematic Sagrada Familia in Barcelona, bring to life the Hollywood sign on Mt. Lee in Los Angeles, create the iconic shell-shape sails of the Sydney Opera House, or the neoclassical outlines of London's Buckingham Palace.

For each puzzle, just join the dots in numerical order to reveal famous places from Istanbul and Athens to Moscow and Arizona. The first and last numbers are slightly larger, in bold, and underlined to help you find the start and be sure when you're finished. The puzzles are arranged in order of complexity, and they will take anywhere from 20 minutes up to a couple of evenings to complete. By the time you get to the end of the book, you will find puzzles with more than 1,000 dots to join.

The numbers are always exactly centered above, below, or to the side of a dot, or touching at one of the four main diagonals to it, so you will always know which dot belongs to which number.

We recommend solving these puzzles using a very sharp pencil so that you do not obscure unused dots and numbers. A ruler can be used to draw the lines, if preferred, but this is not essential. You will find that sometimes it is necessary to go over lines that you have already drawn. If you make a mistake, then just carry on because the line-art nature of each picture is very forgiving.

Once you've joined all the dots, you can color in the resulting image. The perforations along each page allow you to tear out any puzzle, so you could give these to friends or even put them on your wall.

The back pages of the book provide a small preview of each completed image, so avoid looking at these in advance if you don't want to ruin the challenge of doing the puzzles!

Dot to dot has never been more challenging …

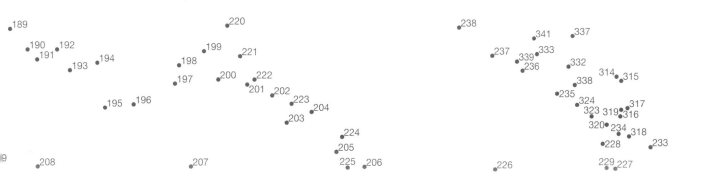

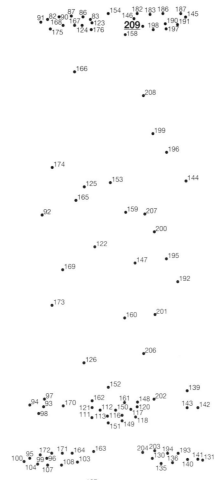

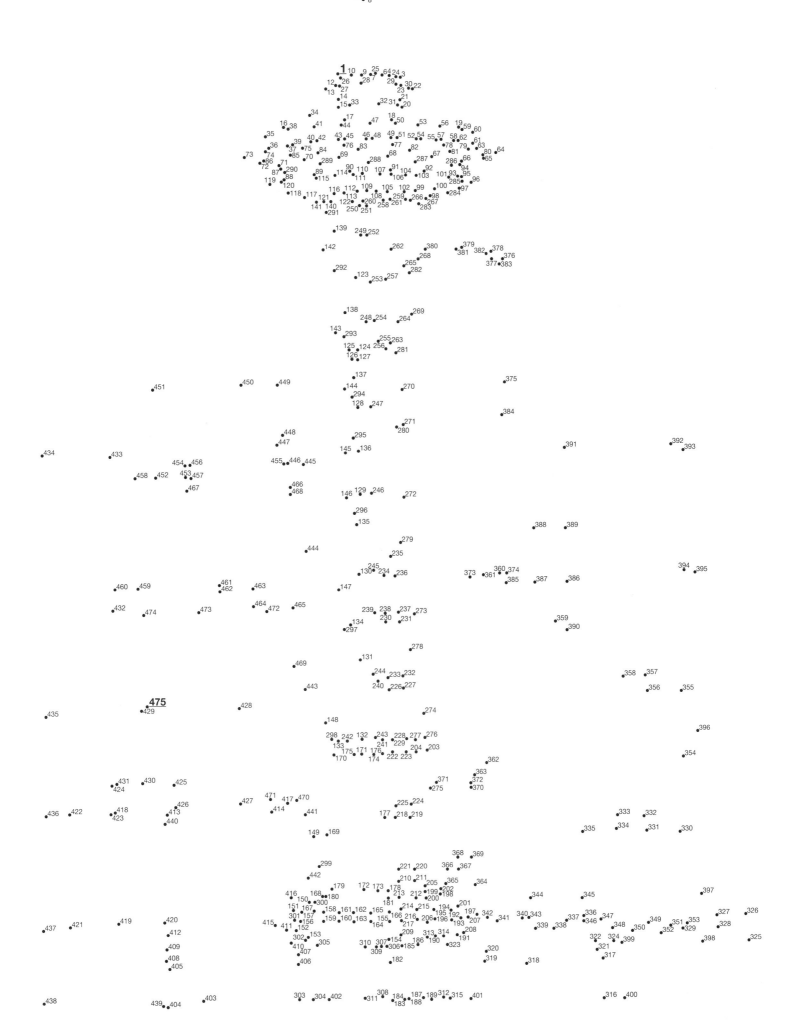

490

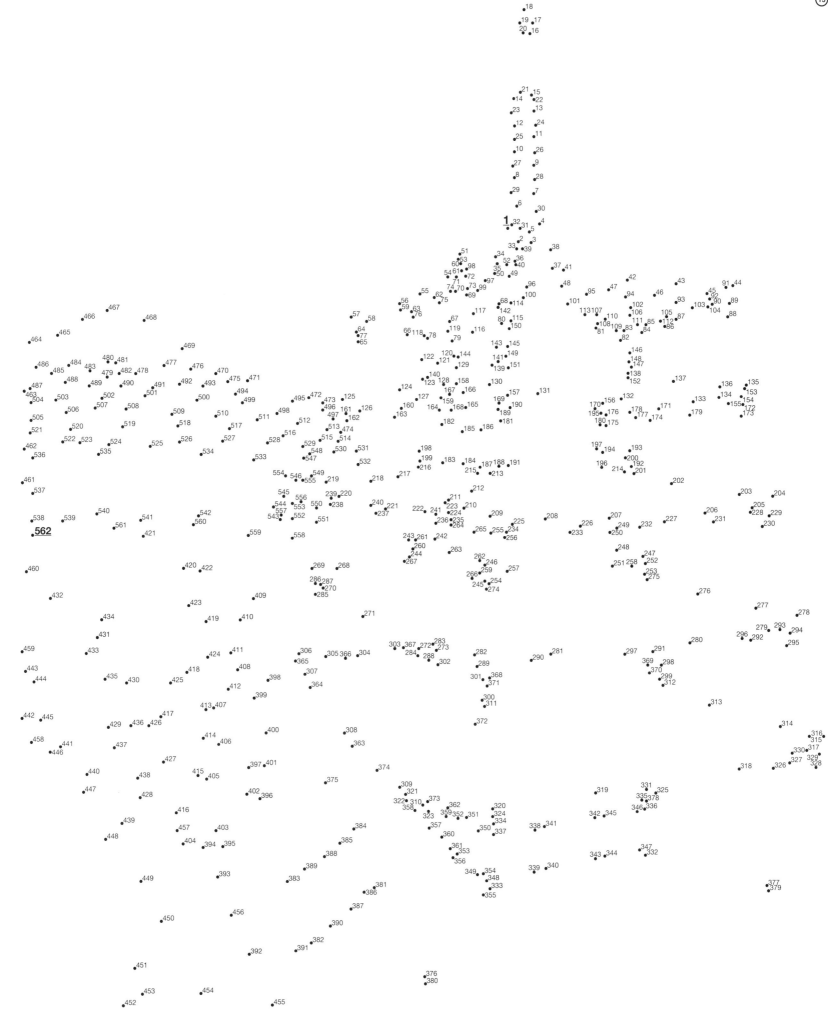

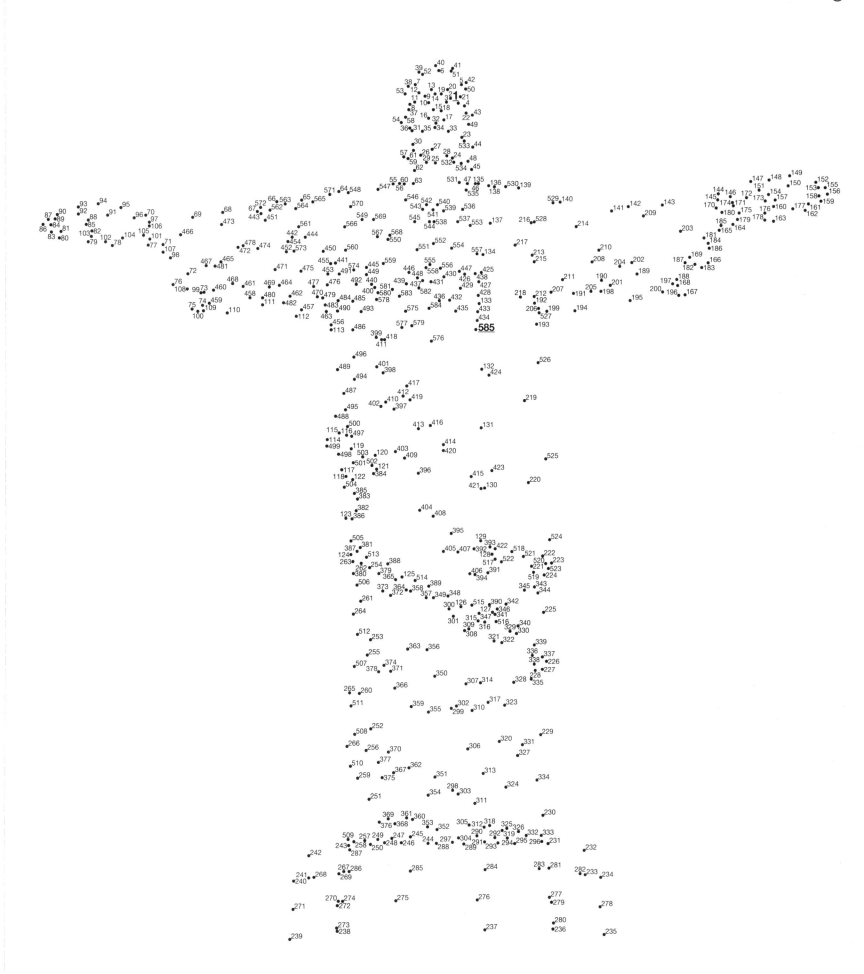

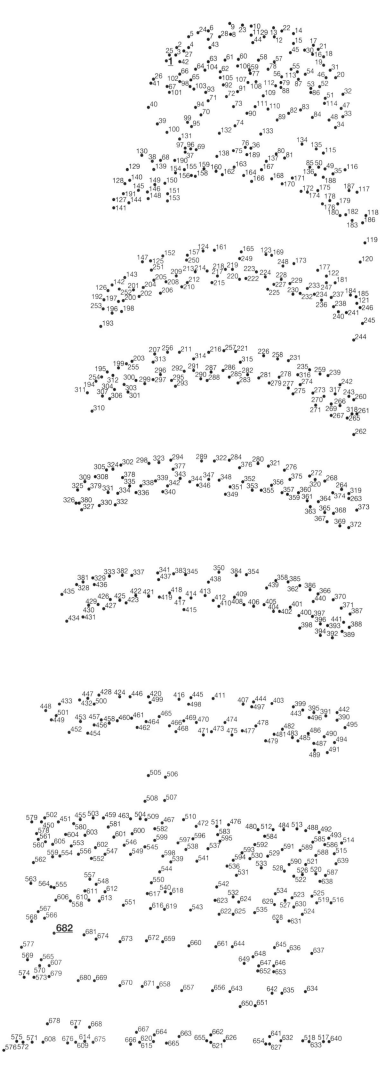

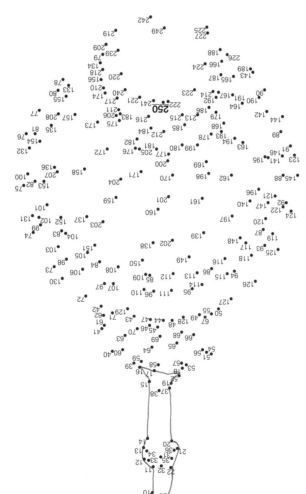

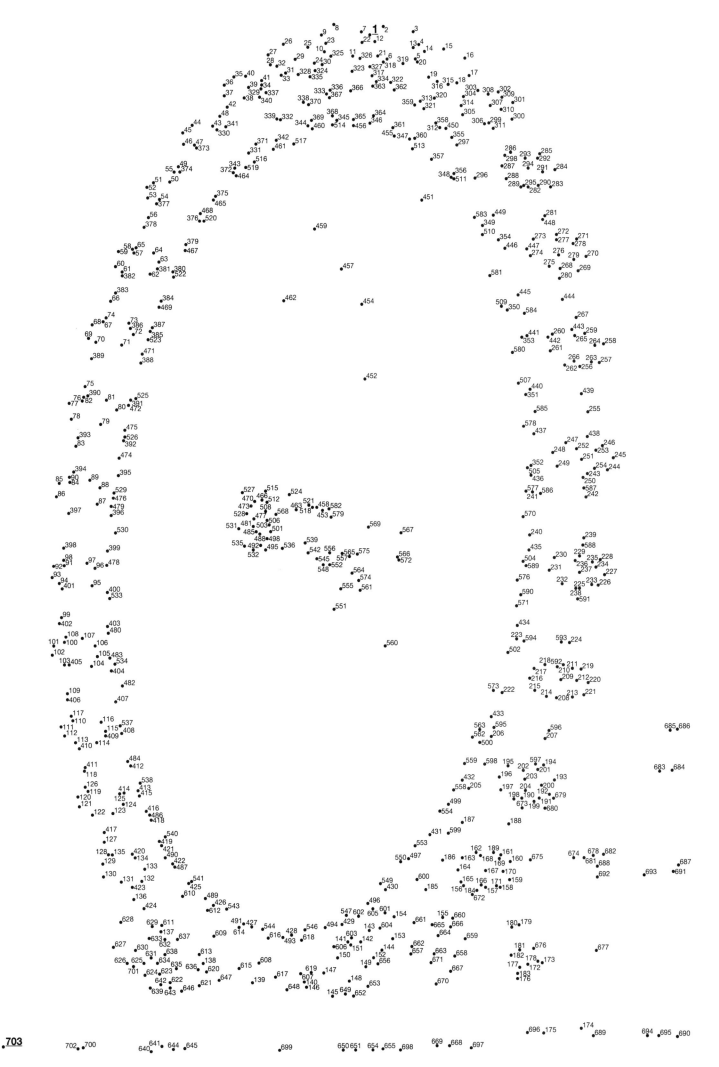

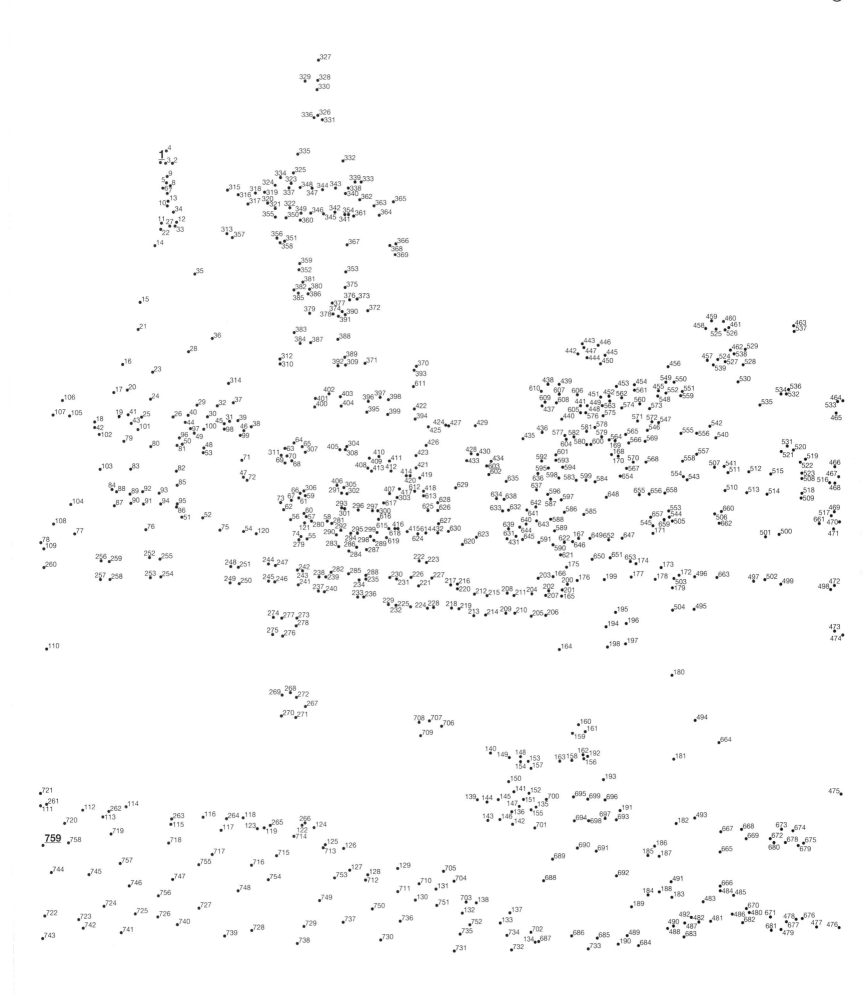

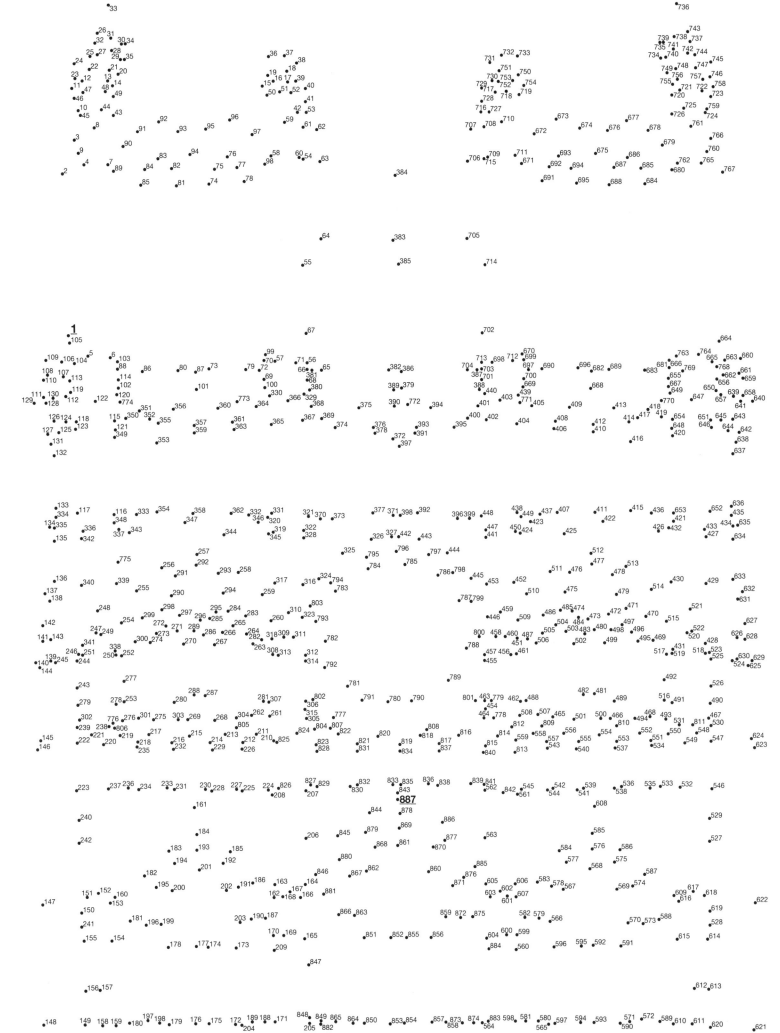

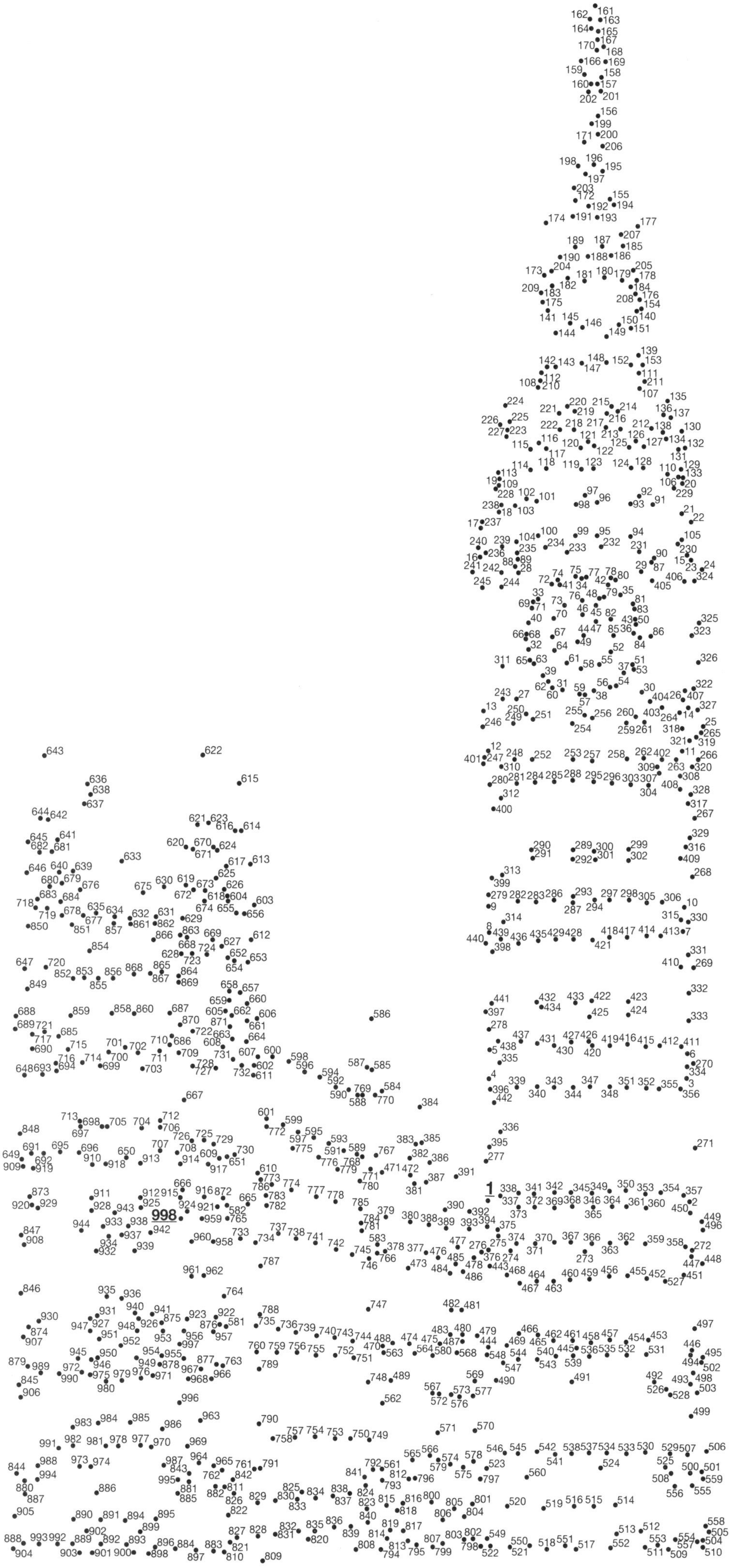

1

1014

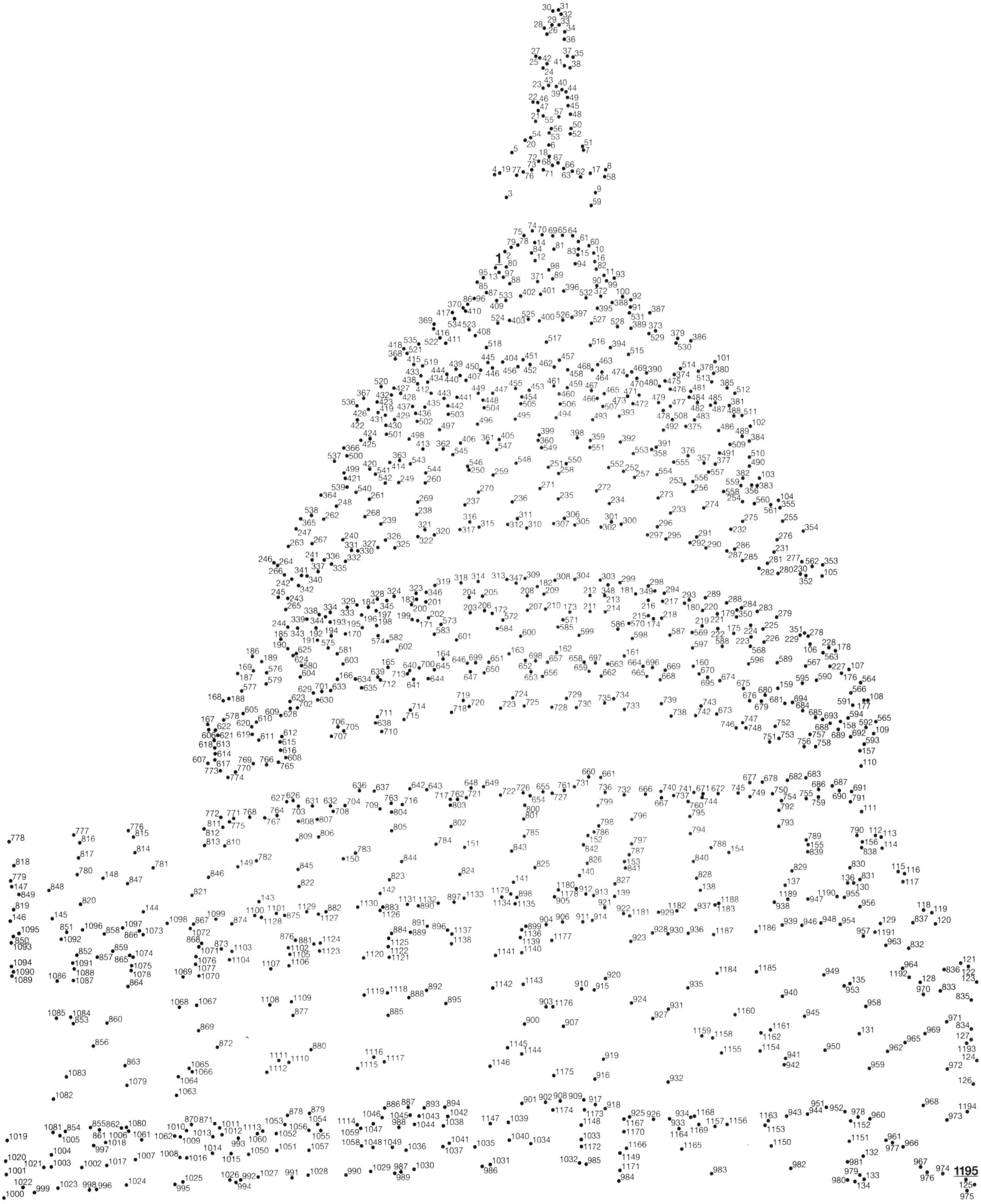

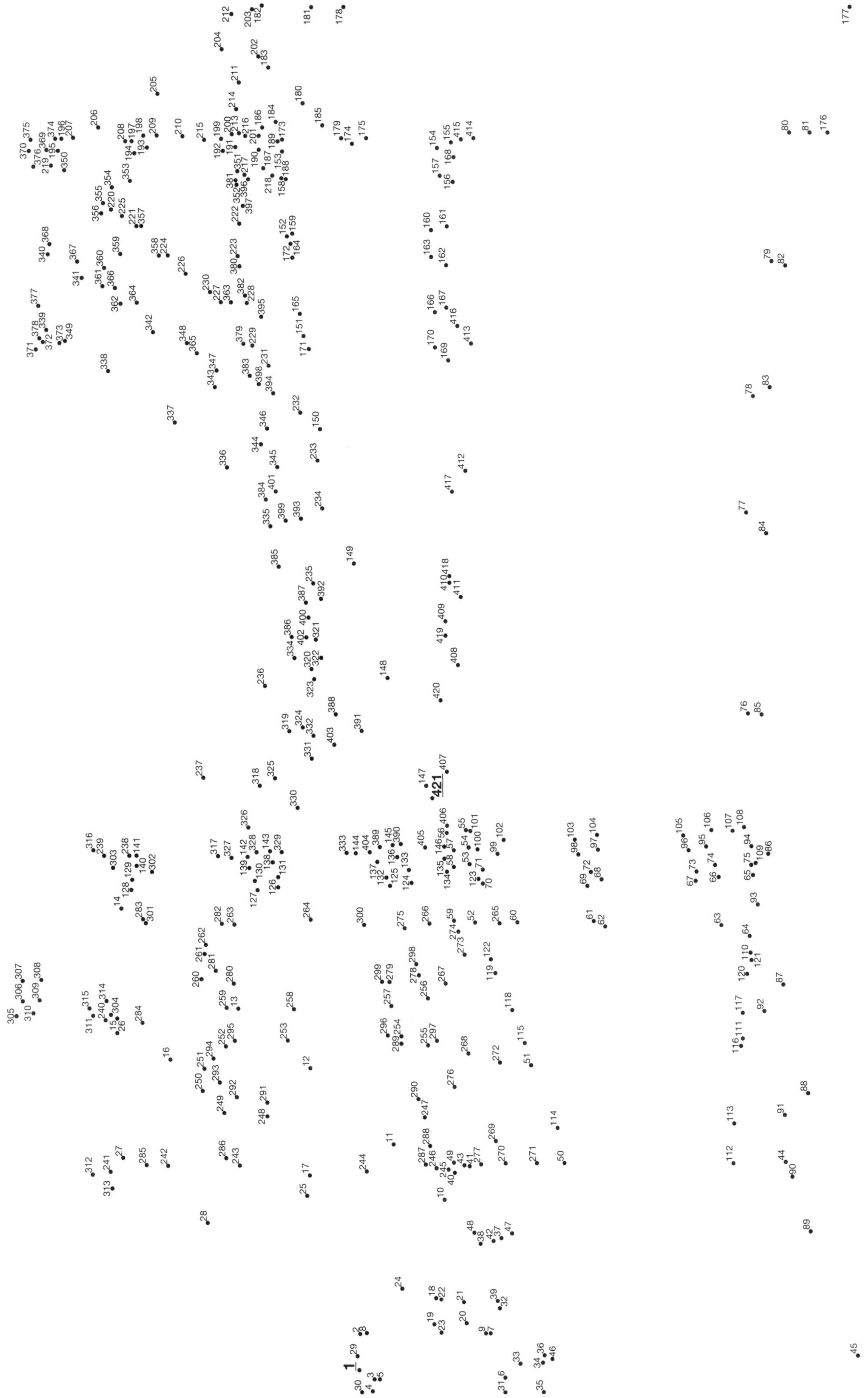

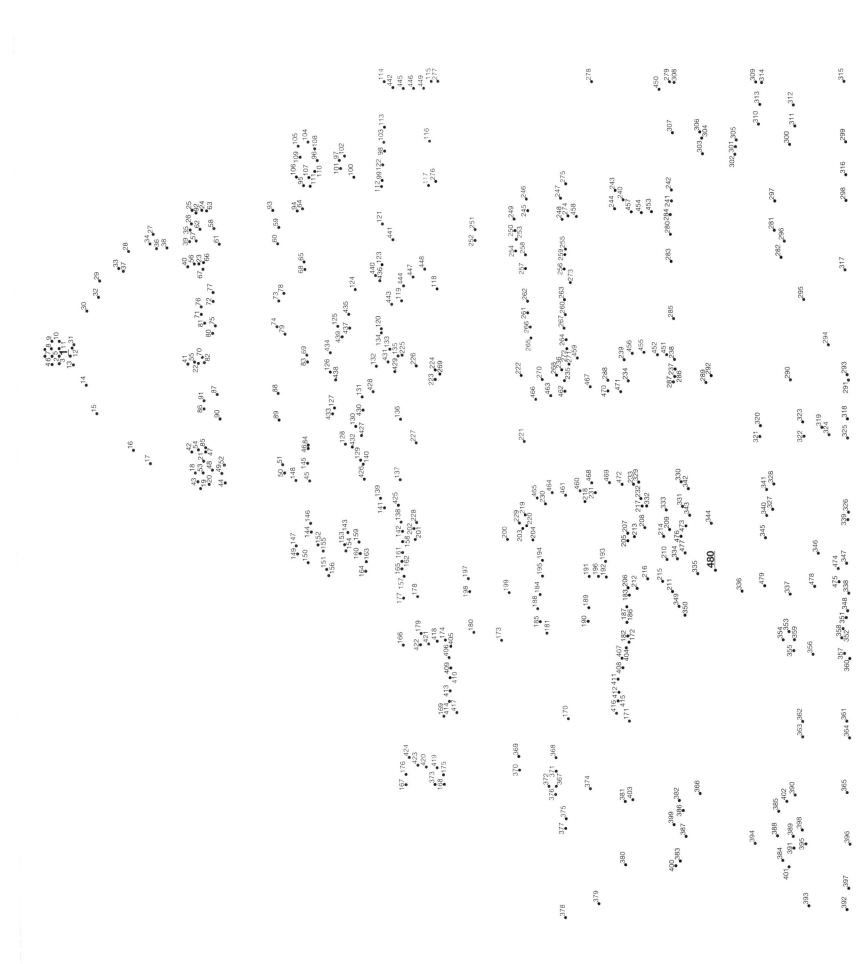

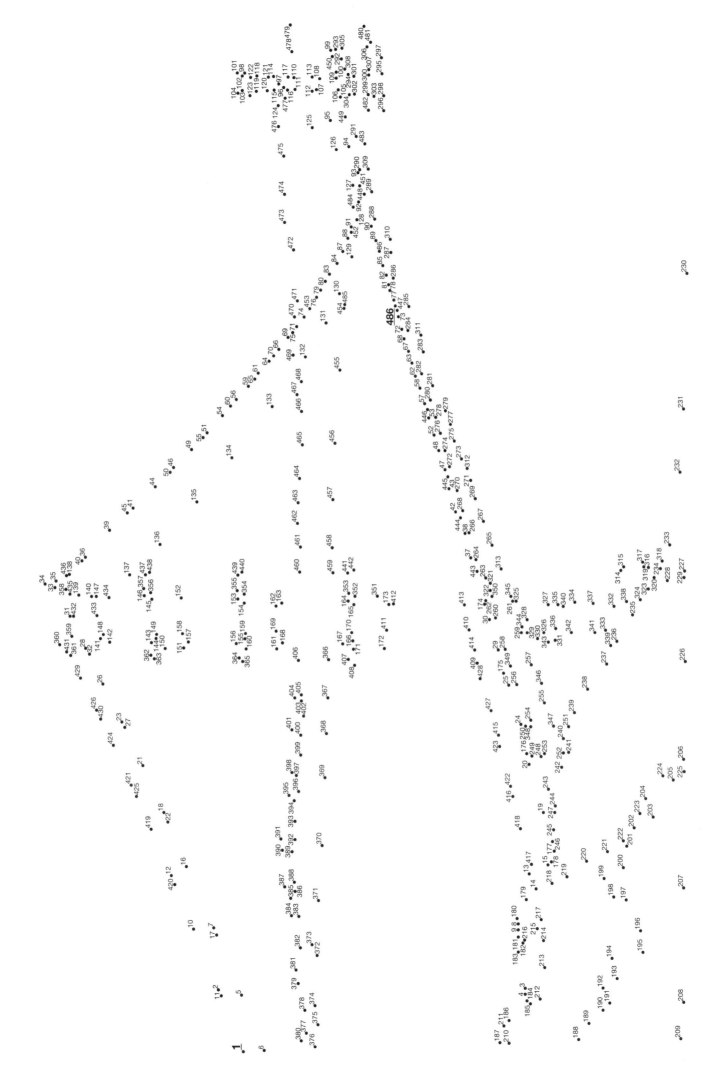

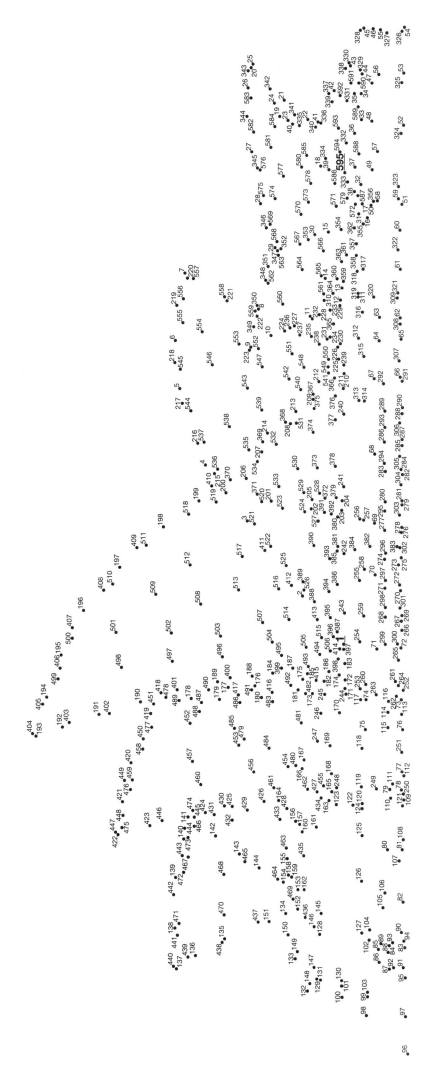

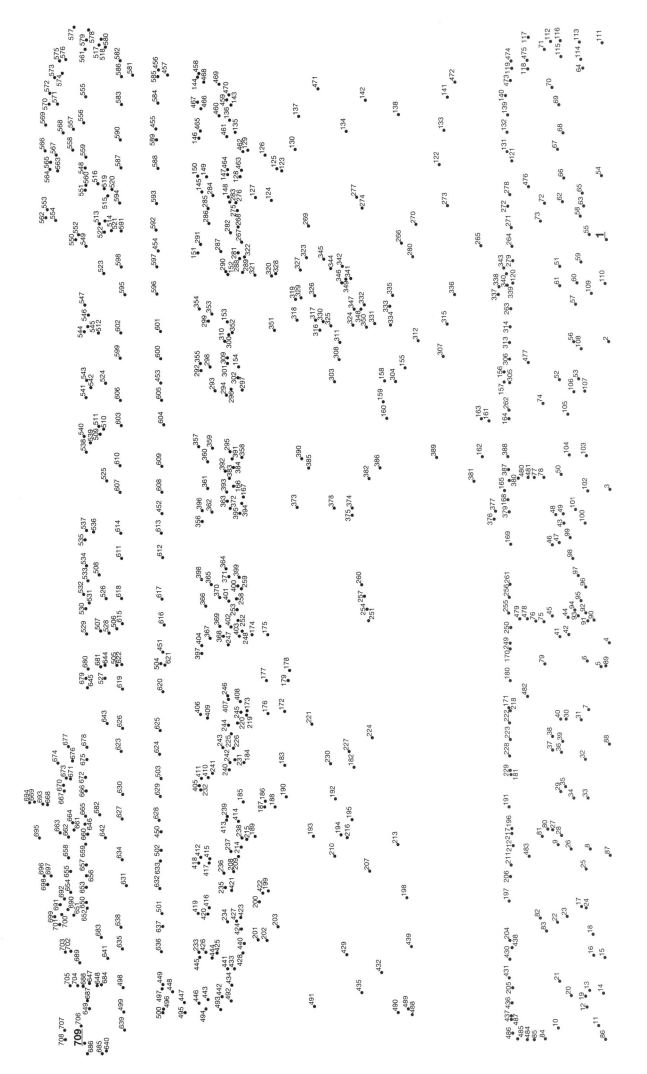

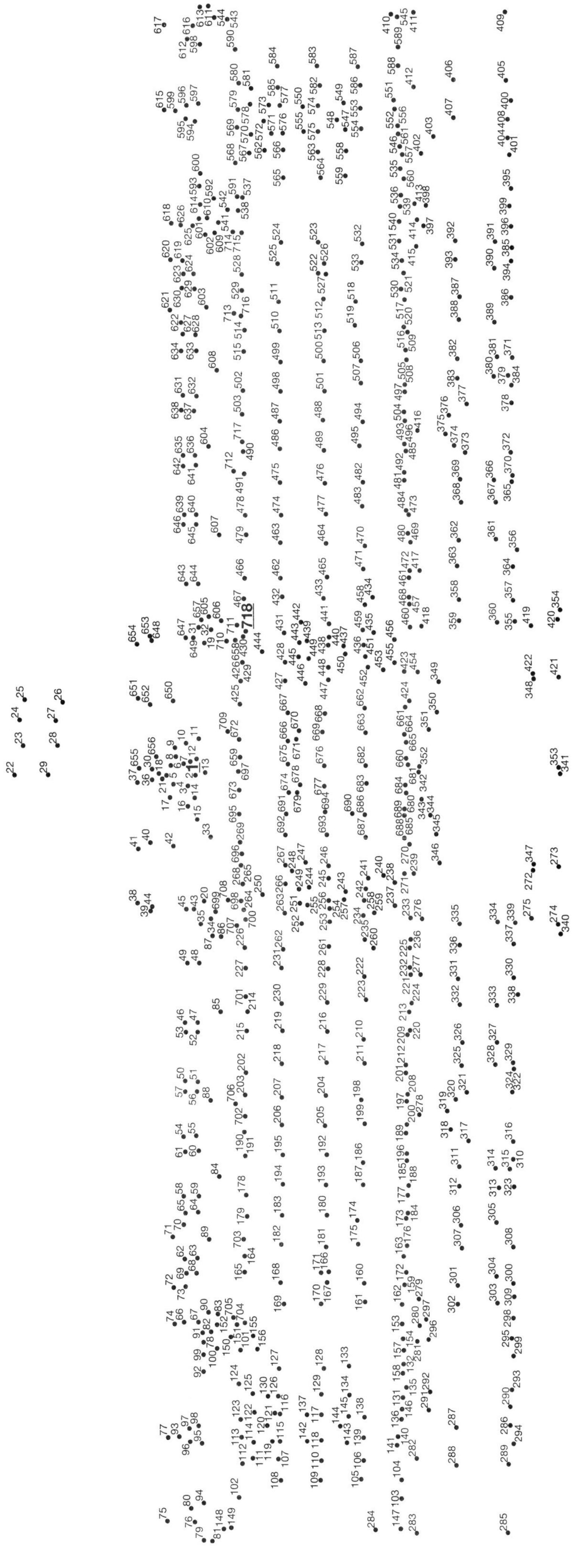

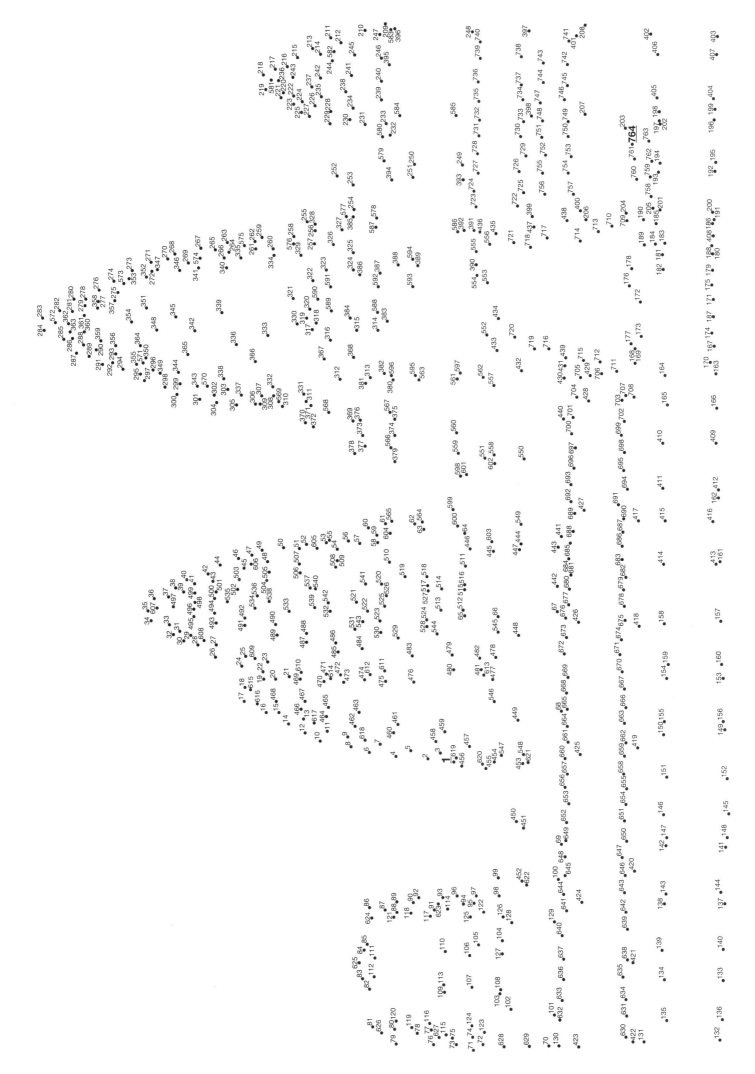

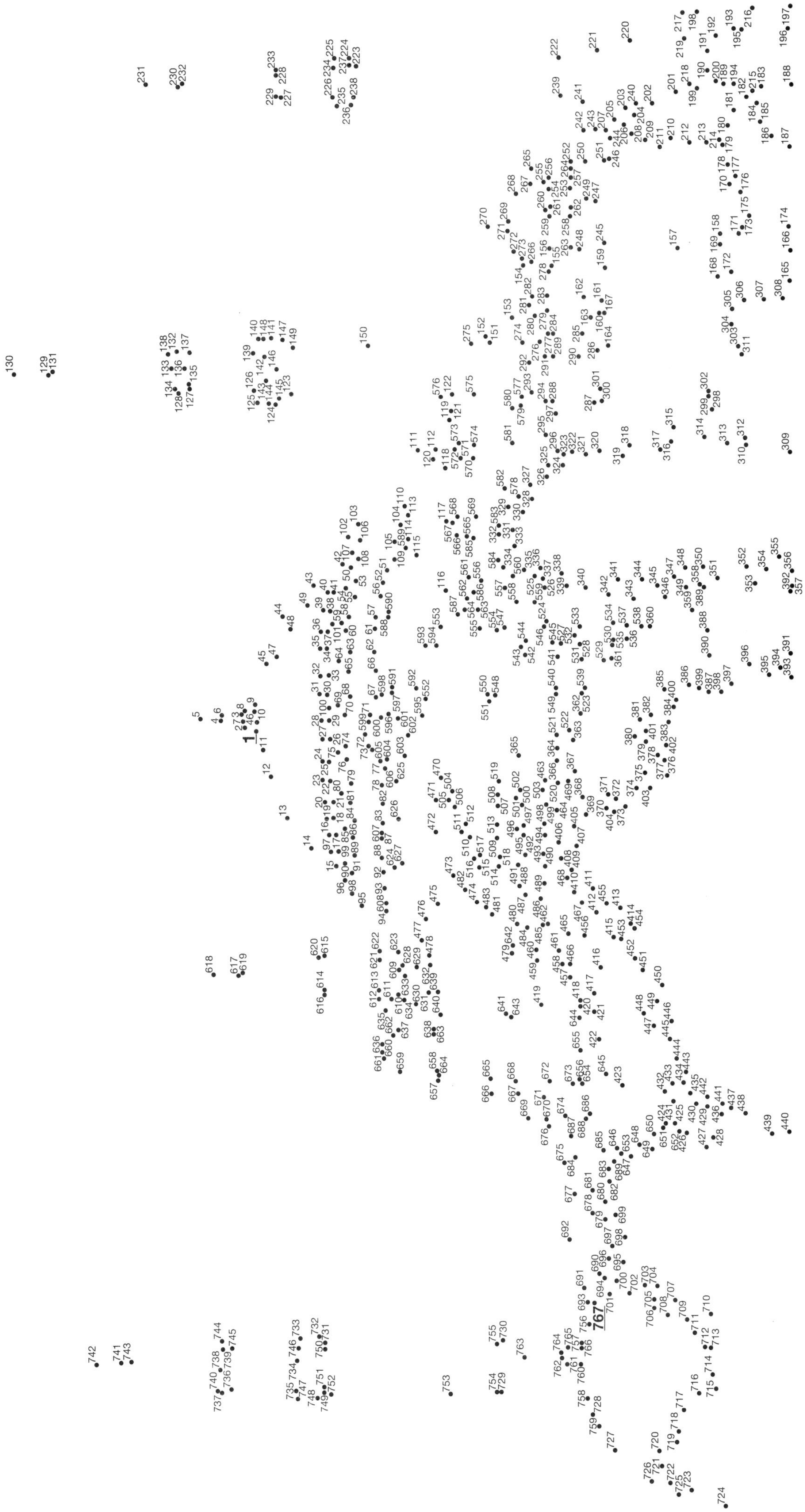

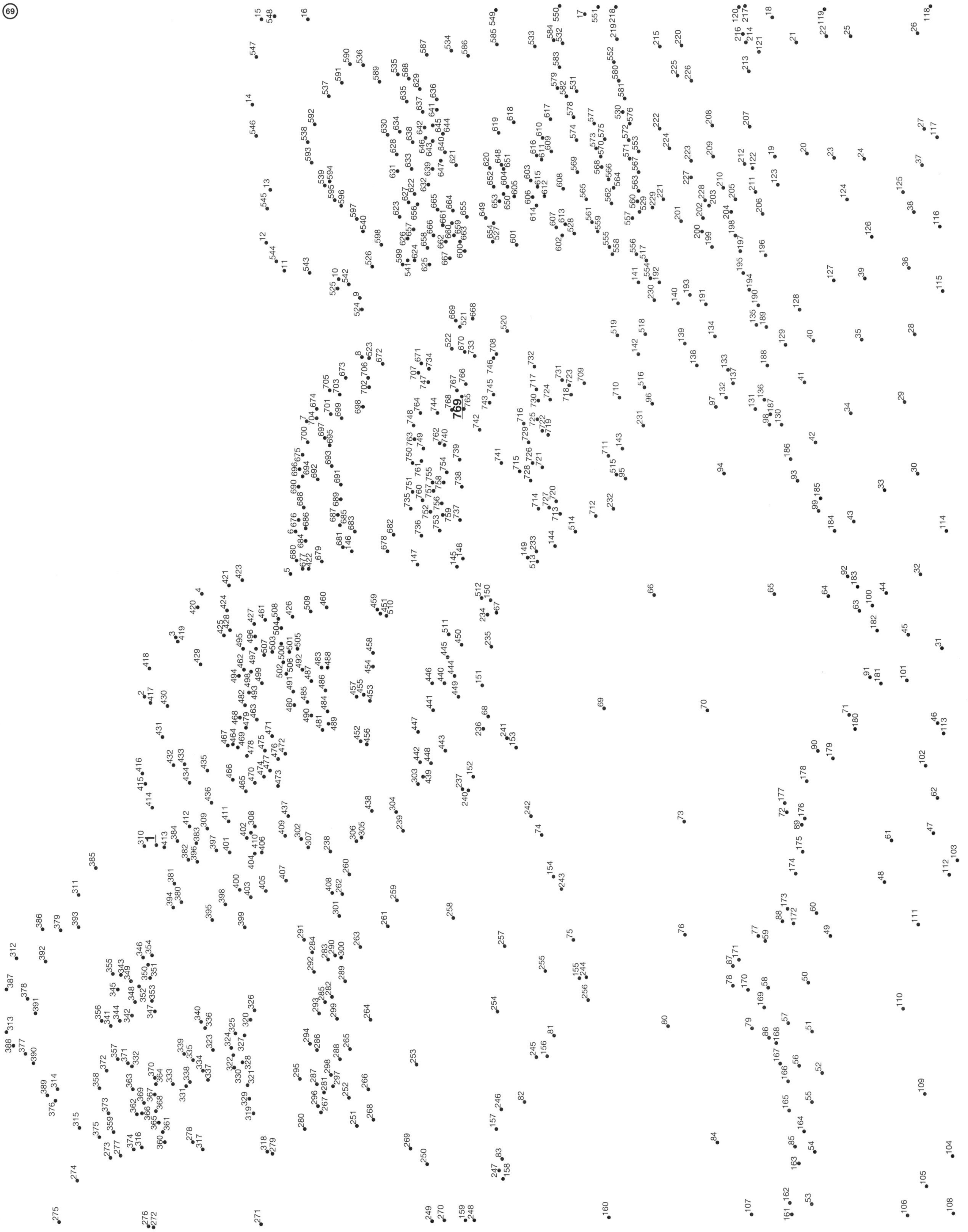

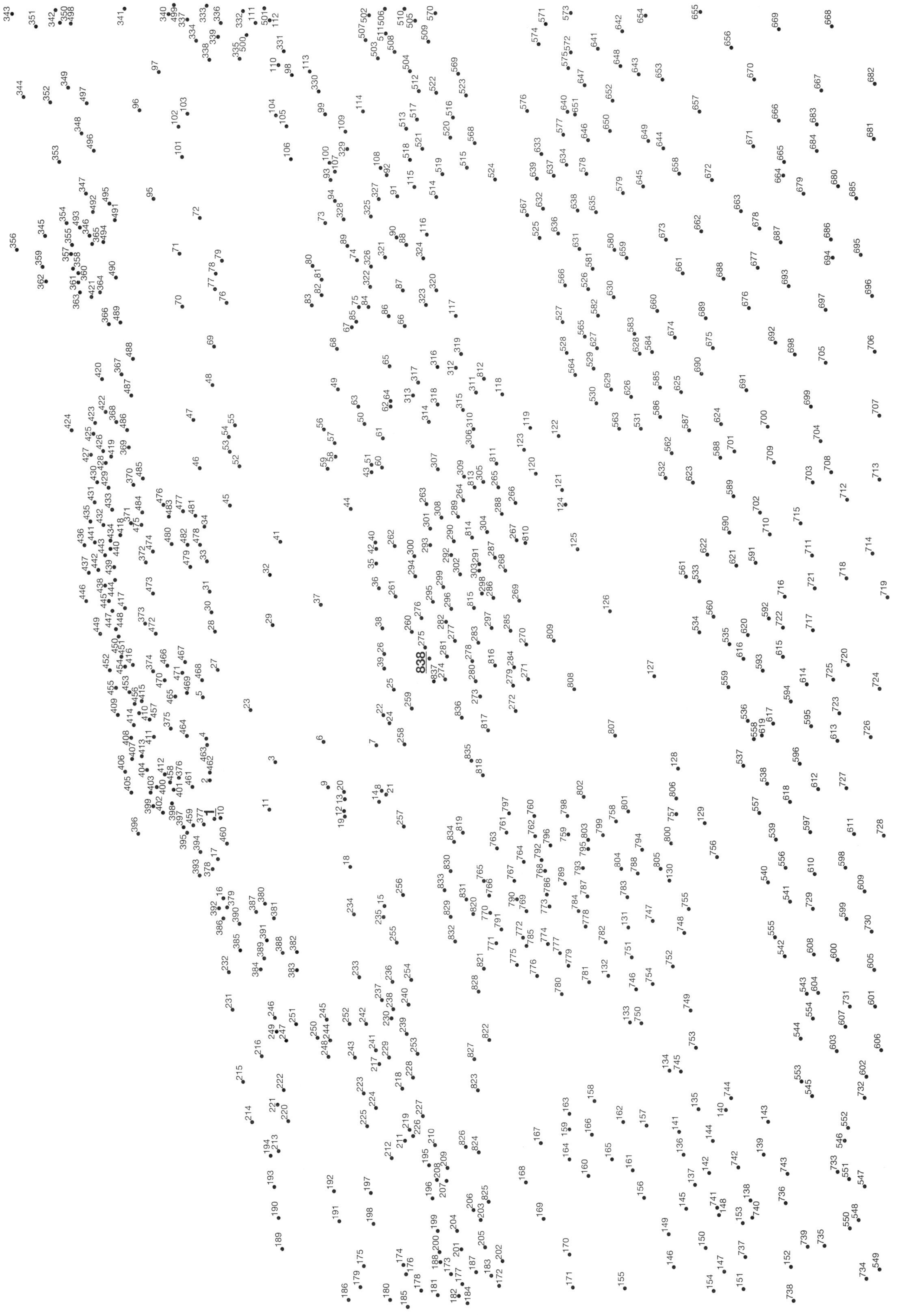

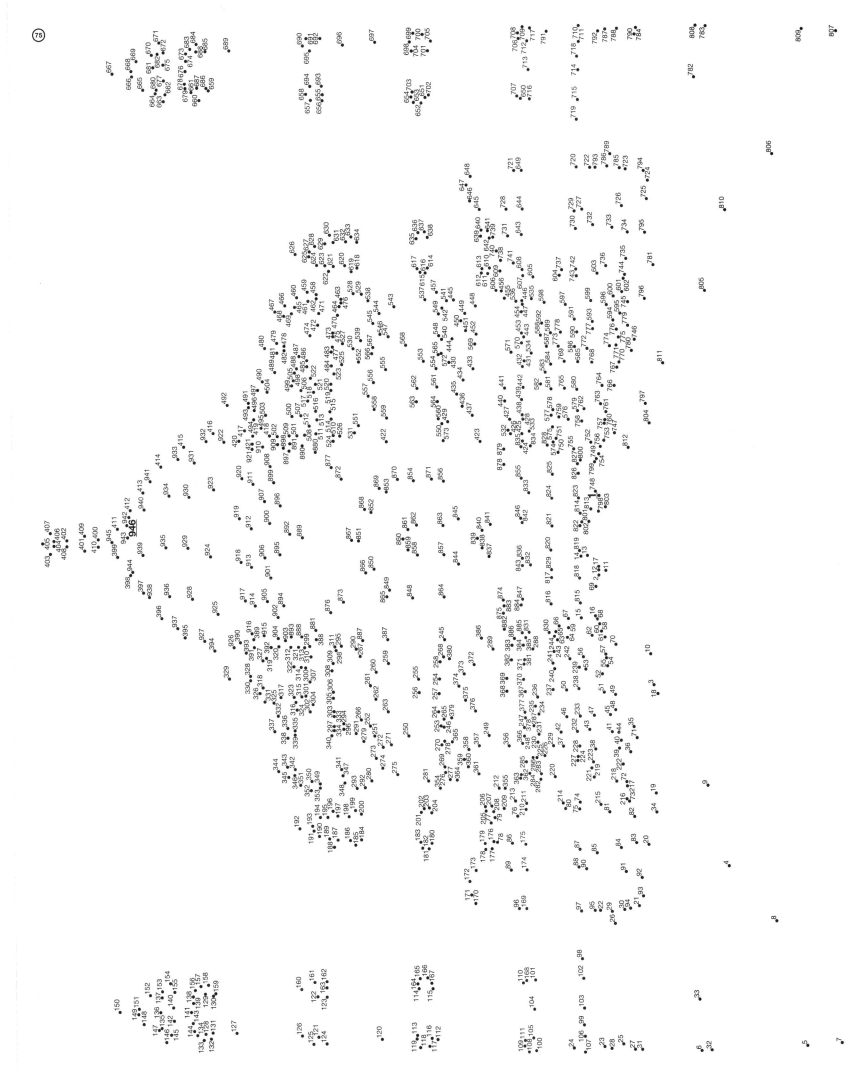

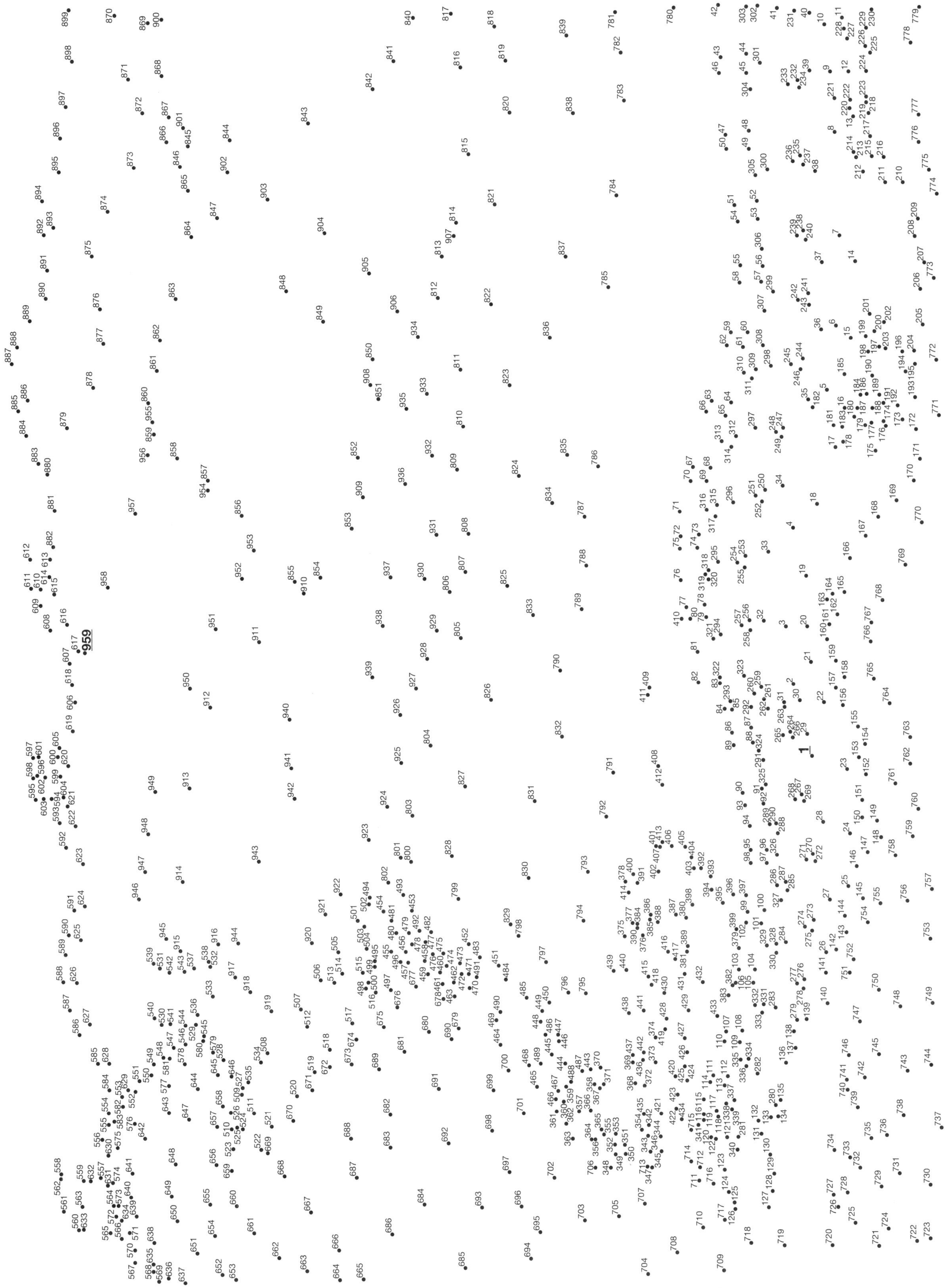

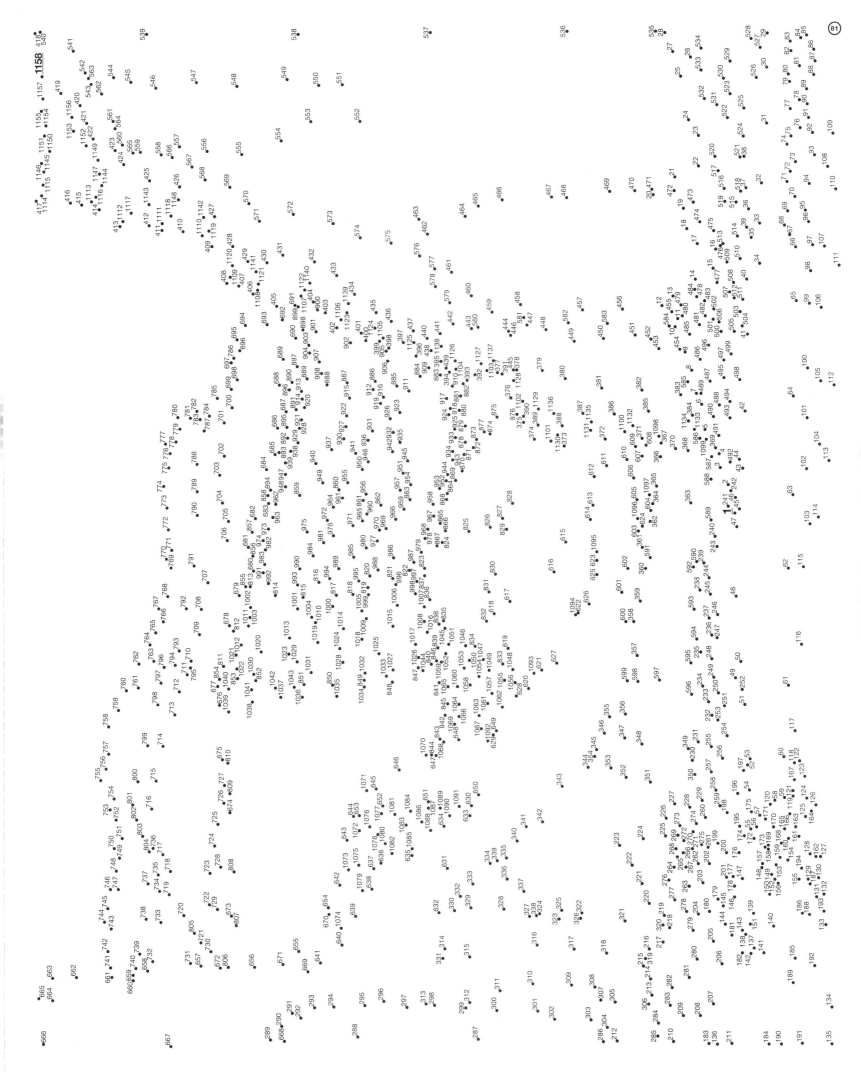

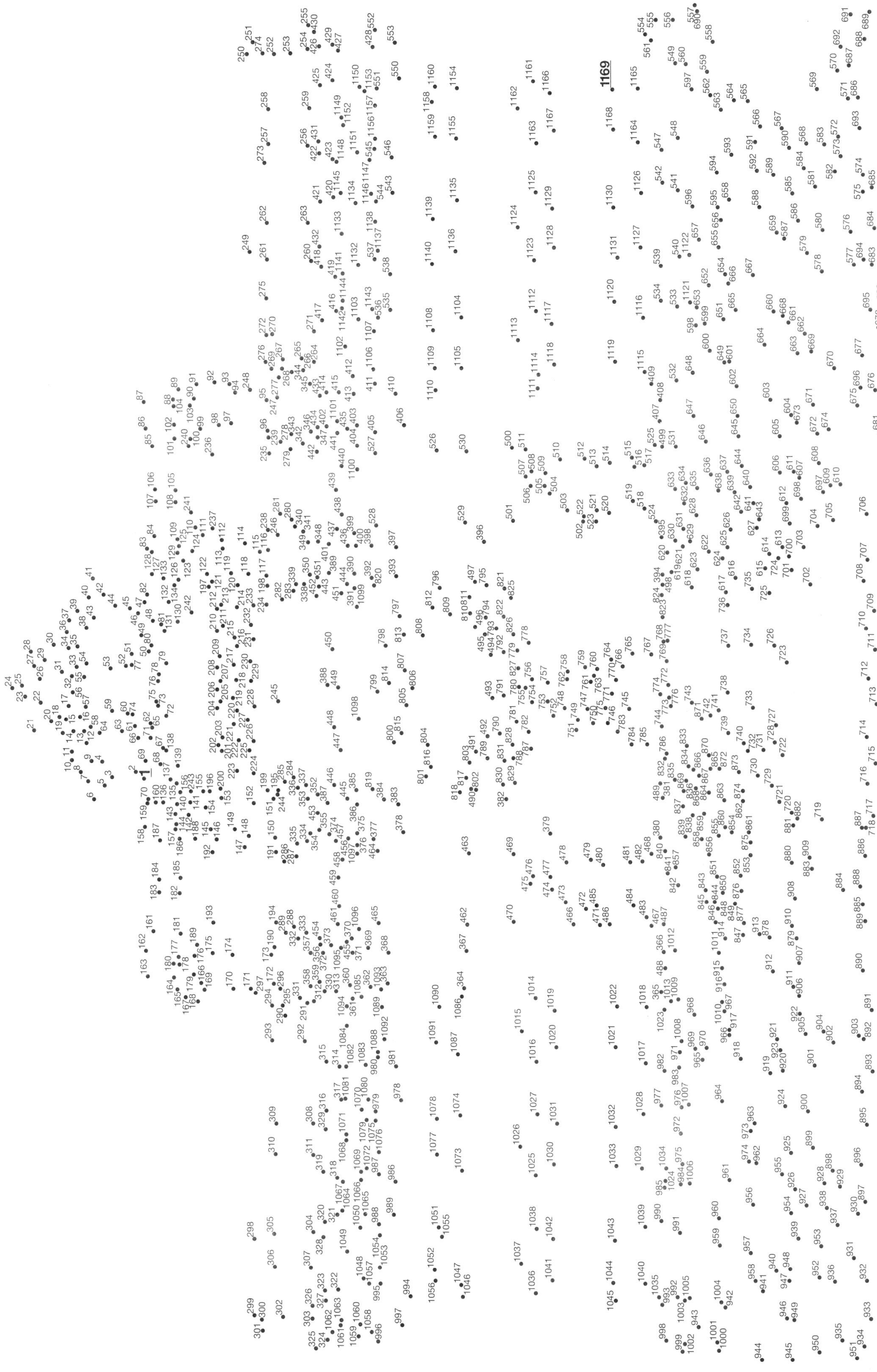

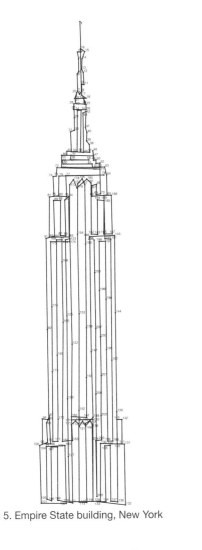

5. Empire State building, New York

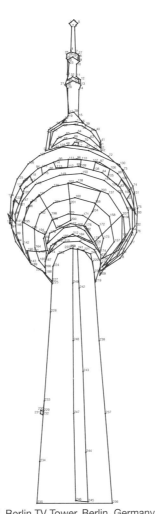

7. Berlin TV Tower, Berlin, Germany

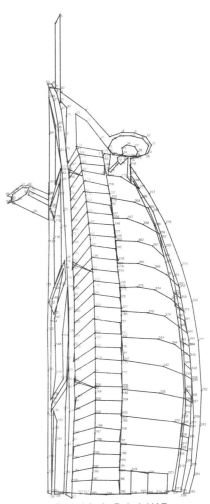

9. Burj al Arab, Dubai, UAE

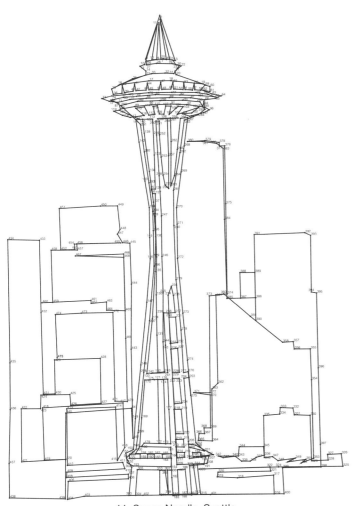

11. Space Needle, Seattle

13. Eiffel Tower, Paris, France

15. Chureito Pagoda and Mount Fiji, Fujiyoshida, Japan

17. Christ the Redeemer, Rio de Janeiro, Brazil

19. Leaning Tower of Pisa, Pisa, Italy

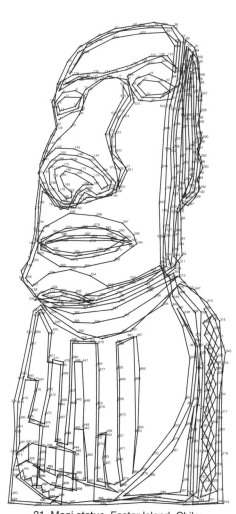

21. Moai statue, Easter Island, Chile

23. London Eye, London, UK

25. Statue of Liberty, New York

27. Bran Castle, Bran, Romania

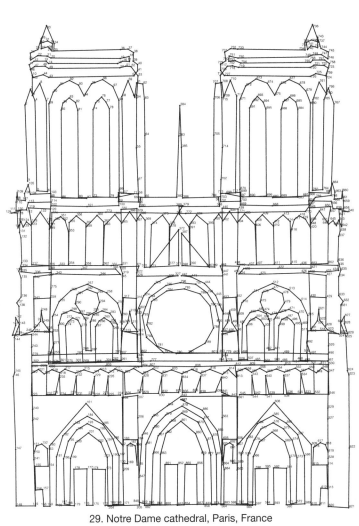

29. Notre Dame cathedral, Paris, France

31. Sagrada Família, Barcelona, Spain

33. Big Ben clock tower and Palace of Westminster, London, UK

35. Saint Basil's Cathedral, Moscow, Russia

37. Great Sphinx of Giza, Giza, Egypt

39. Capitol Building, Washington DC

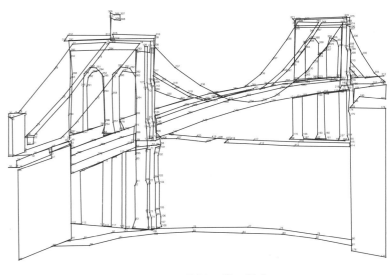

41. Brooklyn Bridge, New York

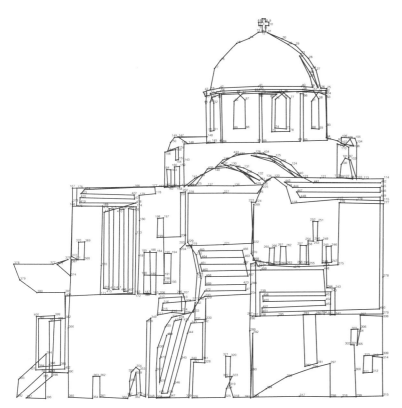

43. Village of Oia and blue-domed church, Santorini, Greece

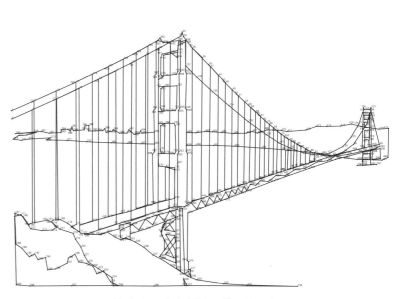

45. Golden Gate Bridge, San Francisco

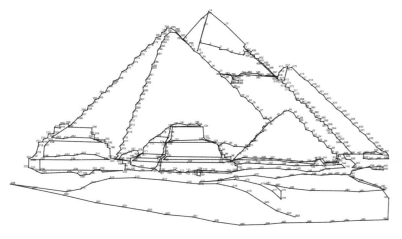

47. Pyramids, Giza, Egypt

49. Stonehenge, Wiltshire, UK

51. Kinderdijk windmills, Kinderdijk, Netherlands

53. Sydney Opera House, Sydney, Australia

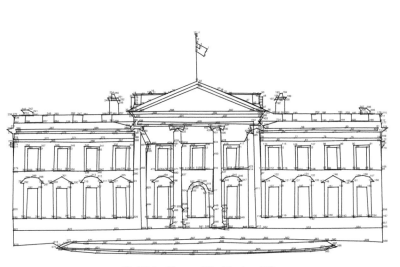

55. White House, Washington DC

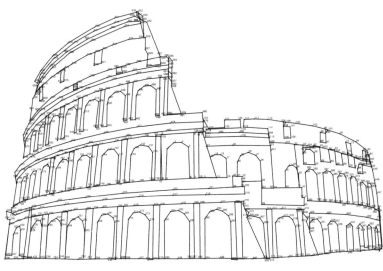

57. Colosseum, Rome, Italy

59. Grand Kremlin Palace, Moscow, Russia

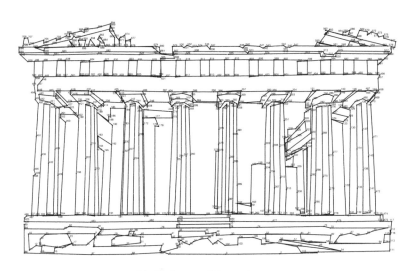

61. Parthenon, Athens, Greece

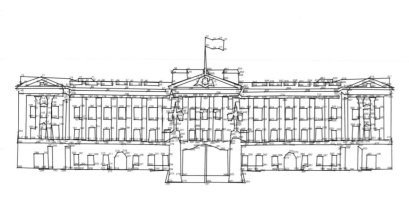

63. Buckingham Palace, London, UK

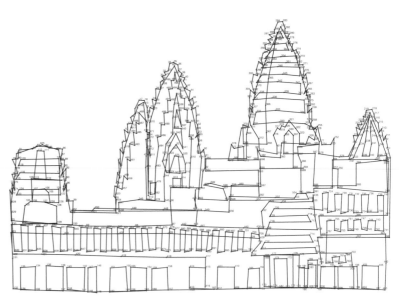

65. Angkor Wat, Angkor, Cambodia

67. Hagia Sophia, Istanbul, Turkey

69. Mount Rushmore, South Dakota

71. Hollywood sign, Los Angeles

73. Brandenburg Gate, Berlin, Germany

75. Taj Mahal, Agra, India

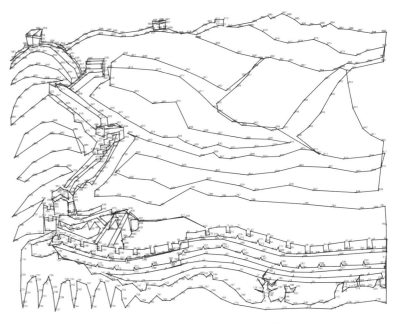

77. Great Wall of China, Jinshanling, China

79. Neuschwanstein Castle, Hohenschwangau, Germany

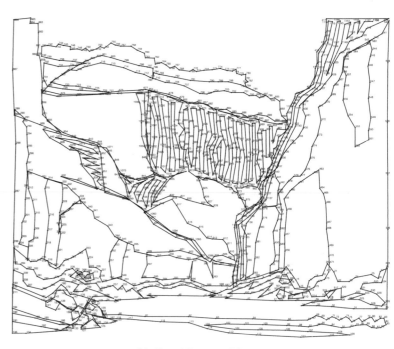

81. Grand Canyon, Arizona

83. Trevi Fountain, Rome, Italy

85. Machu Picchu, Cuzco, Peru